MASK OF THE SENSEI

TITAN
C O M I C S

LEGO® GRAPHIC NOVELS AVAILABLE FROM TITAN™

NINJAGO #1 (3 Oct 14)

NINJAGO #2 (3 Oct 14)

NINJAGO #3 (7 Nov 14)

NINJAGO #4 (7 Nov 14)

NINJAGO #5 (5 Dec 14)

NINJAGO #6 (5 Dec 14)

NINJAGO #7 (2 Jan 15)

NINJAGO #8 (2 Jan 15)

NINJAGO #9 (6 Feb 15)

TITAN COMICS

#2 MASK OF THE SENSEI

GREG FARSHTEY • Writer

PAULO HENRIQUE • Artist

LAURIE E. SMITH • Colourist

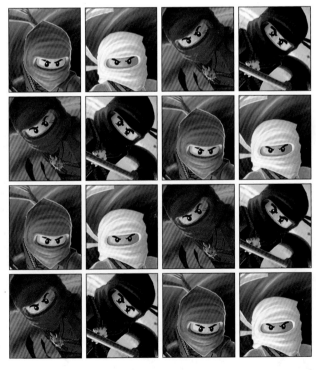

TITAN
COMICS

LEGO® NINJAGO™ Masters of Spinjitzu
Volume Two: Mask of the Sensei

Greg Farshtey – Writer
Paulo Henrique – Artist
Laurie E. Smith – Colourist
Bryan Senka – Letterer

Published by Titan Comics, a division of Titan Publishing Group Ltd., 144 Southwark St., London, SE1 0UP. Contains material originally published in single comic form as LEGO NINJAGO: VOLUME #2: MASK OF THE SENSEI. LEGO, the LEGO logo and Ninjago are trademarks of the LEGO Group ©2014 The LEGO Group. All rights reserved. All characters, events and institutions depicted herein are fictional. Any similarity between any of the names, characters, persons, events and/or institutions in this publication to actual names, characters, and persons, whether living or dead and/or institutions are unintended and purely coincidental. License contact for Europe: Blue Ocean Entertainment AG, Germany.

A CIP catalogue record for this title is available from the British Library.

Printed in China.

First published in the USA and Canada in March 2012 by Papercutz.

10 9 8 7 6 5 4 3 2 1

ISBN: 9781782761938

www.titan-comics.com

www.LEGO.com

MEET THE MASTERS OF SPINJITZU...

ZANE

NYA

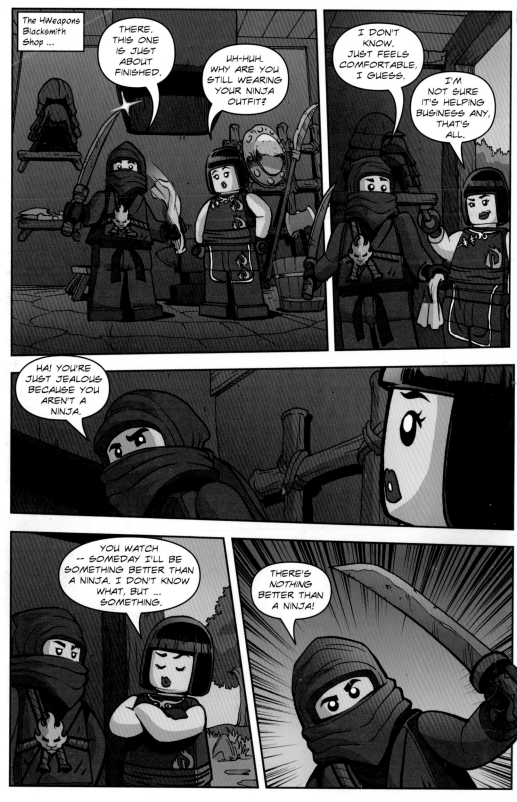

The battle against Garmadon, Samukai and the skeleton army is over.

Samukai's attempt to seize the Four Weapons of Spinjitzu for himself at first looked like it had been a shocking success.

KA-BLAMM

But the power for all four weapons was too much for anyone to handle -- as Samukai found out.

The vortex created by the explosion allowed Garmadon to escape the Underworld, but he has vowed that his battle with Sensei Wu and the ninja is not finished.

Still, for now, there is peace. Kai, Jay, Cole, and Zane have taken advantage of this to return to their native villages to rest before their next adventure.

WE HAVE TO PAY A TAX TO GET INTO THE VILLAGE?

AND TWICE AS MUCH TO GET OUT, YEAH. ALL HAIL THE EMPEROR, AND ALL THAT.

WHAT?! I'M NOT PAYING TO GET INTO MY OWN VILLAGE!

NYA, CALM DOWN. LET COLE HANDLE THIS.

TELL THE EMPEROR THAT COLE, ZANE, JAY, AND NYA ARE HERE TO SEE HIM.

I KNOW YOU! MY KID READS ALL YOUR PARCHMENT ADVENTURES. HE SAYS YOU'RE THE BEST!

THE EMPEROR SAID YOU SHOULD GET SPECIAL TREATMENT WHEN YOU SHOWED UP. GUYS! HEY, GUYS!

MAYBE THE SENSEI IS READY TO BE REASON-ABLE.

OR NOT.

24

THANK YOU, KAI. IT WAS GETTING STUFFY IN THERE. TELL ME, ARE THE OTHER NINJA STILL FREE?

I DON'T KNOW. NYA WAS GOING TO GET THEM WHEN I WAS CAPTURED.

WHAT HAPPENED? YOU'RE YOU, SO WHO IS IT THAT I FOUGHT?

AH, KAI, DID YOU EVER WONDER WHY THERE WAS A SKELETON ARMY IN THE UNDERWORLD?

TO ATTACK OTHERS? NO, FOR THEY RARELY VENTURED OUT OF THEIR DOMAIN UNTIL MY BROTHER GARMADON INSPIRED THEM TO DO SO.

"SAMUKAI AND HIS SKELETONS WERE THERE TO KEEP THINGS EVEN WORSE THAN THEY ARE FROM GETTING OUT."

"WHEN GARMADON UNLEASHED THE SKELETONS ON NINJAGO..."

WHO KNOWS WHAT MAY HAVE ESCAPED?

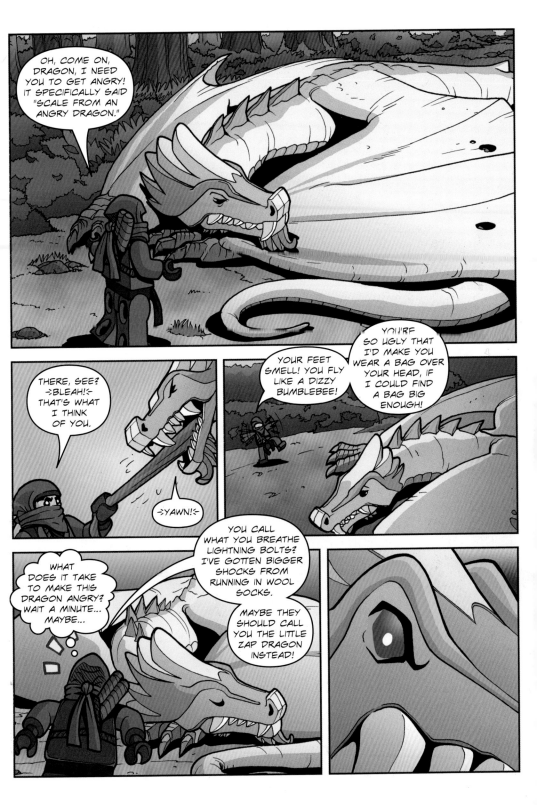

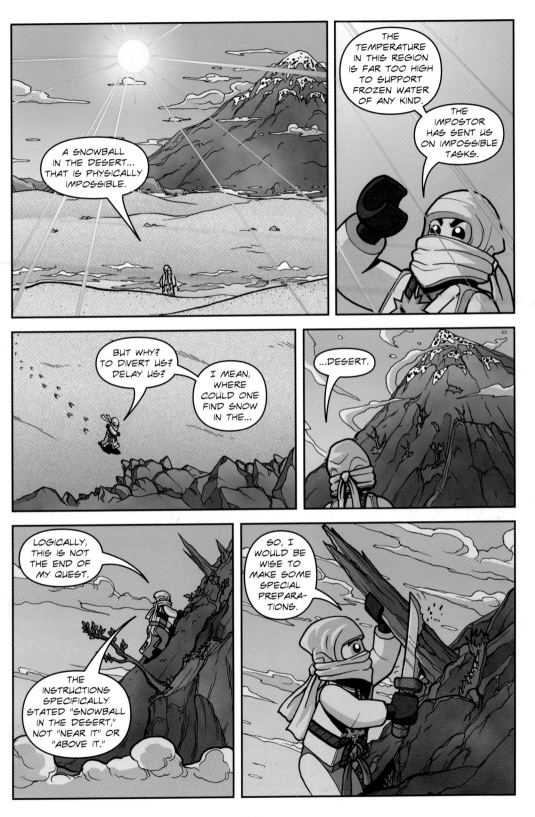

35

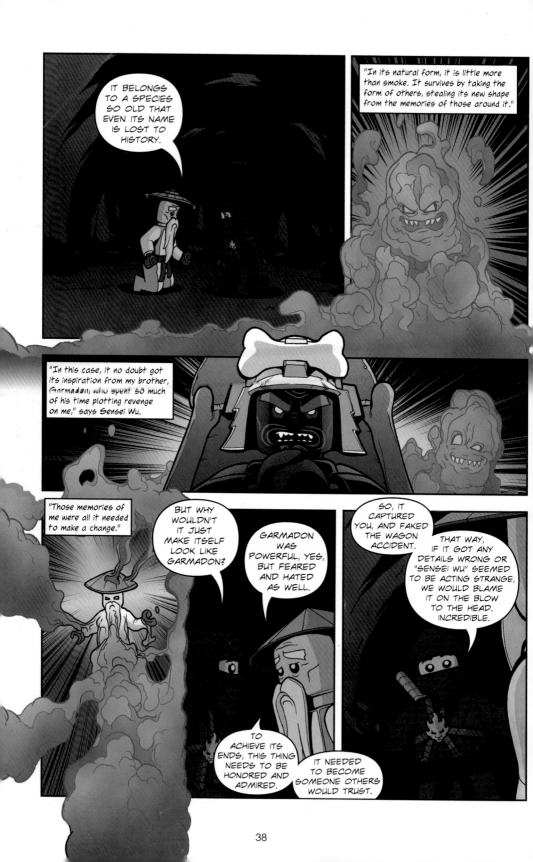

IT BELONGS TO A SPECIES SO OLD THAT EVEN ITS NAME IS LOST TO HISTORY.

"In its natural form, it is little more than smoke. It survives by taking the form of others, stealing its new shape from the memories of those around it."

"In this case, it no doubt got its inspiration from my brother, Garmadon, who spent so much of his time plotting revenge on me," says Sensei Wu.

"Those memories of me were all it needed to make a change."

BUT WHY WOULDN'T IT JUST MAKE ITSELF LOOK LIKE GARMADON?

GARMADON WAS POWERFUL, YES, BUT FEARED AND HATED AS WELL.

SO, IT CAPTURED YOU, AND FAKED THE WAGON ACCIDENT.

THAT WAY, IF IT GOT ANY DETAILS WRONG OR "SENSEI WU" SEEMED TO BE ACTING STRANGE, WE WOULD BLAME IT ON THE BLOW TO THE HEAD. INCREDIBLE.

TO ACHIEVE ITS ENDS, THIS THING NEEDS TO BE HONORED AND ADMIRED.

IT NEEDED TO BECOME SOMEONE OTHERS WOULD TRUST.

41

46

QUICK, WE HAVE TO-- WAIT A MINUTE, WHERE DID IT GO?

I DON'T KNOW.

IT HAS CHANGED ITS FORM AGAIN, TO SOMETHING TOO SMALL TO BE EASILY SEEN.

GREAT, AND ME, WITHOUT MY *FLY SWATTER!*

FROM WHAT THE SENSEI SAID, IT NEEDS THE ITEMS WE COLLECTED. SO, IT HAS TO FOLLOW US!

THEN LET'S GET GOING! HEY, WHERE'S NYA?

WE HAD ANOTHER MISSION FOR HER AFTER WE LEFT THE VILLAGE, SO SHE'S--

OH, YOU SENT HER TO OUR DESERT HIDEOUT WITH THE ITEMS YOU COLLECTED. GOOD IDEA!

HUH?

Where is Nya? Far from the desert, as it turns out...

TIME TO COME IN FOR A LANDING.

49

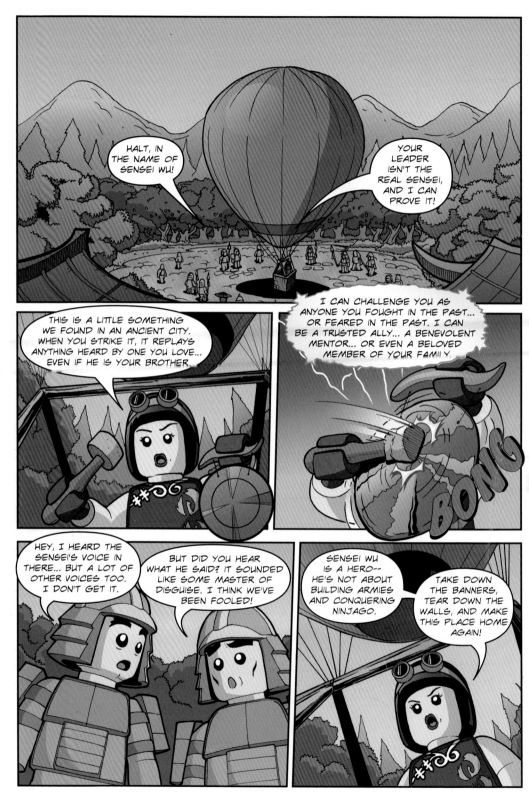

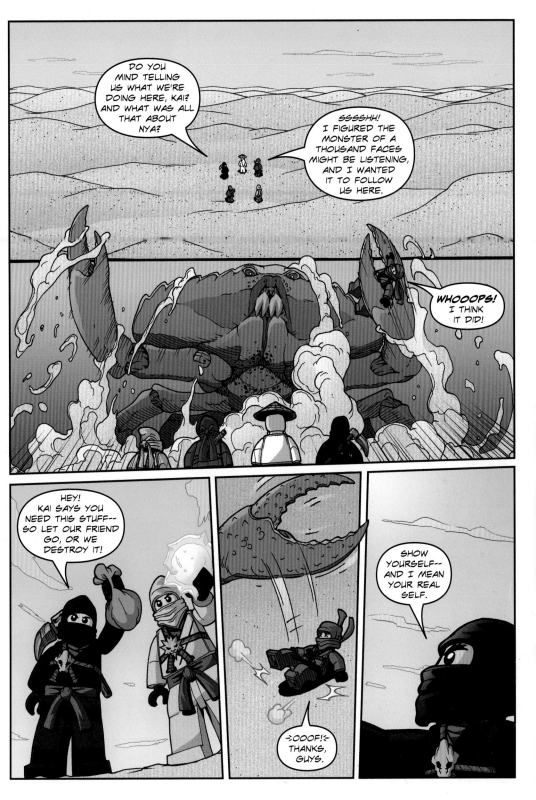

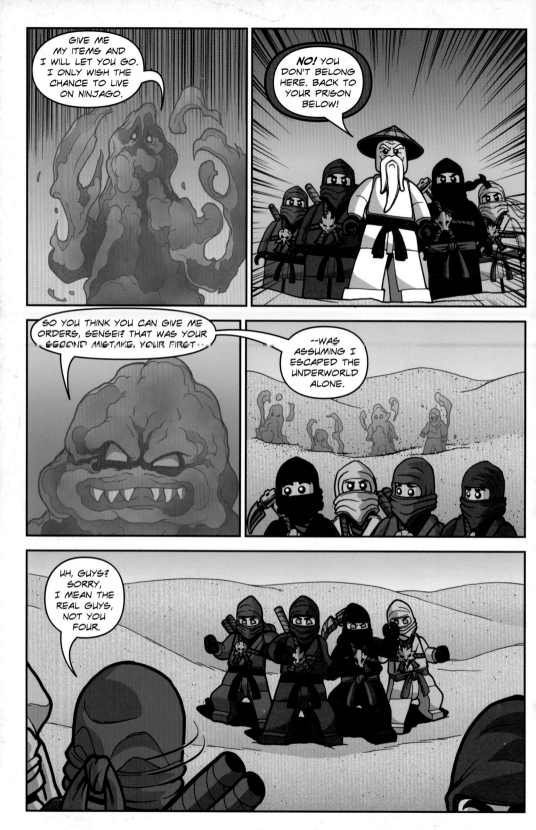

56

LET'S HEAD BACK TO THE VILLAGE AND GET NYA.

SENSEI, DO YOU THINK OTHER THINGS MIGHT HAVE ESCAPED THE UNDERWORLD WHEN THE SKELETONS WERE HERE?

IT IS POSSIBLE. BUT THERE ARE OTHER MENACES ALREADY HERE...

CREATURES WHICH, I HOPE, WILL REMAIN SEALED AWAY FOREVER.

WELL, THAT SOUNDS... OMINOUS.

IT MIGHT BE WISE TO TELL US OF THESE THINGS, SENSEI, SO WE CAN BE PREPARED.

THERE ARE SOME THINGS, MY NINJA, THAT ONE CAN NEVER BE PREPARED FOR.

ONE MUST SIMPLY SEE THEM FOR HIMSELF.

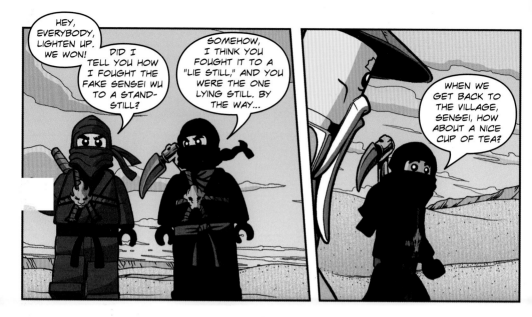

SENSEI WU
ACCEPT NO SUBSTITUTES!

MEET THE MASTERS OF SPINJITZU...

JAY

COLE

ZANE

KAI